DIVINING FOR STARTERS

Also by Carrie Etter

The Tethers
as editor, *Infinite Difference: Other Poetries by UK Women Poets*

Divining for Starters

Carrie Etter

Shearsman Books
Exeter

First published in the United Kingdom in 2011 by
Shearsman Books
58 Velwell Road
Exeter EX4 4LD

http://www.shearsman.com/

ISBN 978-1-84861-150-4

Contents

I. Landed

II. Erotics

III. Divining

for Claire Crowther

ESTRAGON: Sing something.

VLADIMIR: No no! (*He reflects.*) We could start all over again perhaps.

ESTRAGON: That should be easy.

VLADIMIR: It's the start that's difficult.

ESTRAGON: You can start from anything.

VLADIMIR: Yes, but you have to decide.

Samuel Beckett, *Waiting for Godot*

I

Landed

Divining for Starters (2)

considering human cell division

that piling days indicate toppling hours

here the cellist raises her bow

(what now on the leaf)

and fifty years ago schoolchildren rolled mercury over their desks

isolate and social

divining for starters

which stone drives the ripple

going for circumference, provision, and jasmine

another delicate startle

on the rancid plateau

Divining for Starters (18)

The small stand of trees now quickened by a gale, each leaf
    losing its discrete

And again a rest that resembles languor for the light
    nearing noon

The unseen, sunseen work of chlorophyll I know and don't
    know proceeds

The reflexive work of the body apace despite its seeming
    reticence

Yet I linger on the tree as though it alone

And again a rest that resembles languor for the light nearing

McLean County Highway 39

tar shrugs goes to dirt
gravel's slow crunch over
winter with no hill for
frost to the horizon

*

green hectares rising into
Illinois' no blond endeavour
but for the corn tassels dangling
covert silk threads

*

cycle up dirt-dust's brown haze
flattening thought a prairie
the only height for miles
a grove its doe

*

sweat and cornstalks taller than
pushed through the close
click into speed sticking hairs
peel the nape free

*

all exhale the green expanse
cicadas' two notes sunset
the red eye pink strata
push an unwavering line

*

without thought three miles out
an idle porch swing
shrug or flattening not silence
but nothing heard in

*

soybeans crouch along even as
horizon at my back
cools toward streetlamps and cement
glide in the last

Prairie

sprawling through night   a train's low horn
the crossings   empty   the drivers' ritual
maintained   reflex or   especial precaution

do the sleepers hear it   do their ears
make unconscious record   to litanize

a prescience without particularity   unbound
on prairie   to vague expectation
with or without   hope

with or without   the train whistle's
thread   reminder redeemer

of silence   each isolate mind
banked in prescience   if it's not nostalgia
impalpable   in small hours   impalpable

in the drift   as names ease from objects
unmannered ritual   especial   withoutness

Treeline

What meets behind the trees

(it is the arc of a sigh)

what must, what does, what may

(from the floor tiles of would-that-I-were-not)

faith or science or

(the vice must be adjusted to allow movement without escape)

the shortest article in world news: a new planet, perhaps

(the swum line)

that aery sustenance

(the arc, as in the degrees of perception)

one assuaging glimpse

Seed

in the echoing roar of a childhood

retreating, advancing, how good is your sense of

the years spatially distributed, a swatch of graph paper

the entrancing right margin

dizzying, defying focus as one might (not I)

try to count the remaining verticals

a mockery of _____, the traipse around the sundial

coming now to the strange harvest

of withered, of milk-brown, of dead stalks, the next crop

from this crackling soil, these brittle grains

Invalid

The fluctuations, paced to startle. When scrappy flowers pocked the field, nostalgia was in the making. By fluctuations, understand the gradual adjustment to a new status quo, say a metallic taste, tuna casserole on Thursdays, shortness of breath. *You know how it is,* or so goes the refrain. In retrospect, boredom becomes bliss. There's the chance that if you don't succumb to the swerve, you'll crash. Some days you can almost smell the mildly unpleasant odor that stained your hands after you cast the last houndstooth daisy aside; you might be able to conjure it, you think, if it weren't for. *You know how it is.*

Paternal

A parent a plinth. The first week he regarded hospital as hotel. So the variables include the kind of stone, its consistency, the velocity of prevailing winds. What's purer than an infidel's prayer? How strangely, in the second week, the swollen limbs stiffened. And the effects of climate change: milder winters, more precipitation, two, three heat waves each summer. All American, non-Jewish whites are Christian by default. Incredulous, I realise his bicycle may rust and walk it to the shed. Such an ordinary act of reverence. The pulmonologist, the neurologist, the family physician. A bed is a bed is the smallest of bedsores. Blood doesn't come into it. Ritual, of course, is another matter. A Midwestern town of that size exhibits limited types of architecture. I've yet to mention the distance. Come now, to the pivot, the abscess, another end of innocence. In every shop, the woman at the till sings, "Merry Christmas," a red turtleneck under her green jumper. I thought *jumper* rather than *sweater*, a basic equation of space and time. Midnight shuffles the cards. Translated thus, the matter became surgical, a place on the spine. Each night the bicycle breaks out to complete its usual course. A loyalty of ritual or habit. "ICU" means I see you connected to life by wire and tube. A geologist can explain the complexities of erosion. The third week comes with liner notes already becoming apocryphal. Look at this old map, where my fingers once stretched across the sea.

Orange County, Year Five

for James Zeigler

would it were by degrees recognized
as a glutinous advance
but there was no
deceiving the Midwesterners

with hills and eucalyptus
(the manifest negative of another,
an implacable year)
divested of unsought glamour

the palm treed shore
seagulled and beguiling
our name's elliptical orbit
inconsiderate of landscape

and forced to resuscitate it
silo whether or no

Alaskan

for Jason McKenzie Alexander

1. Fireweed

Purpled cluster thrust

    —a parade an attentive throng—

rising away quick green mountain yields

and fir fully erect   (the hard last freeze)

a moose nods   fireweed by scent or sight

    (lumber toward)

his great mouth
yank the stalk from unbroken

ineluctable pull.

2. The Kenai River

breadth—rightly Alaskan—figures we have—
magenta bells up,
three, four, five feet—

acres—

a range   seamless cloaks
                  one by one junco-frail

pervades a narrow where no one
the nets the salmon
figures we have (or name).

3. The Fisherman's Memorial

blue-bronze grants the sea
      wave a fiercer wield for
the stolid. An impossible
          —the rope thus larger in proportion—

IN MEMORY OF
BUNNY WE MISS
ALWAYS YOUR WIVES

     draws across the landed

at vigil, his rope ever poised, ever still

4. The Flats: A True Story

the fine silt the suction   (the tide out, the flats calm)

     the bride in the sublime:
     fir-dotted and sea

she laughs exclamation
point.
     grins the silt's tremendous
       her legs a millimeter one
         at a time pull,
       scoop scoop around

        and the tide—

5. Valdez Exhibit

over where you live
to scale 600 square miles to cover
slick the feathers
drums into steep the banks
in the black   *run aground . . . in case*
you want to know
cover the place she breathes

6. Anchor Point

across the bay
and they'd no compass rods tackles

merged with the open
the rain splinters and the wind

The swells
the boat's belly down between waves

one leg in the rain

hollered for direction   we pointed into fog

bowed and slackened and bowed again
bounced through

Our rods drew   the rain the white

Rod by rod, the fish
and eased them into the bucket

7. Painting the Marsh

Compose nearly satiated
by late and before it, the thinning
its magenta
the weeds' dense roots

withers, winter
the year's apex to freeze there clutch
the mud the mosquitoes

Almost satiated: amorphous swathes of
persist among fuller and at the marsh's edge
sunstruck and quiescent
practising for

Cormorants atop   (get this right)

Divining for Starters (36)

in the death-wish, in the end of beginnings

the river placid with cold, oh I know winter

the broken stalks, a field of parched stumps

what volition's in seasons, in renewal

the wind at its coarsening, at the mill

into the core, whose arrested depth

the hard ache of it, into or against which

or wait, the dull grievous wait

Estate Management

from Christine de Pizan's *The Treasure of the City of Ladies*

war or crusade leaves behind

manors, fields, and fieldhands

how ladies who live on ought to

all the responsibility of administration (revenue)

by persuasion the details and a standard of living

at the study of lease and contract—*nothing dishonourable*

nothing dishonourable in *familiarity*

to oversee (revenue) servant, sheep, furrow

to market to market to sell a rich

to preclude undersight, i.e. deception (loss of revenue)
    (poor prices)

sometimes renders more profit, e.g. the Countess of Eu

felt no shame in the *perfectly* respectable work

profit (nothing dishonourable to women)

Poem for Two Voices (3)

What I know

is what you lost

what I lost

what we lost

in the climb

in the transatlantic flights

the degrees of separation

numb guilt a little

numb me

sure enough

my hand handled no axe

but deforestation

another ozone baby

fool

how ascetic should I

dream on

what can I

you're too late

please

don't go home

but

don't go home

for the first few feet the river

cars candy computers

shallow but then

cows crops—curtains!

the abrupt plunge

beyond your limited imagination

I try

shucking your guilt

I try

fool

give me one species one

ecosystem

I could try

to fix it?

admit the anthem is a dirge

II

Erotics

Divining for Starters (53)

the body's warmth more palpable for

flavour of those grapes

outside speech a quiet pub

fingers on the well-worn grain soft as

no general objection to metaphor

and now under my breasts the slightest

fingering my small store of words

held on the tongue

the skin of the flesh of it

that low precipice

Divining for Starters (67)

in the suppressed gesture

of desire, if only

gazes join, more wire than bridge

soft under the chin

as if to transcend by travel

fingertip fingertip

Any Given Summer

here   though unexpected

        absolution's spectrum

   touch where

simplifying   a thicket of stars

    what you see

   the tongue's velvet   touch

      by pointing by bringing

at the fingertips   not to rush

   choose one and point   light

the membrane of it

    touch tongue to   stars

set to   and yet surprising

   redeemed by   just see it

at your fingertip   touch

   in the starry field   just

on our tongue

Two, Post-Pastoral

Forsaken the bed, forsaken the wine
for an earlier, post-pastoral year,
an indivisible will, my neck aching
to hold this starry gaze

                      all the while
forsaking the high ground for more secure
a consistency of delectation

                           clearly you see
one or another problem; I wait on your
flowers scentless or pungent, there's no
making a bouquet of the two

                             it's all about two,
two breasts, two tongues, two
rattling attics

              up in the storm of
pliable stem

Subterfuge for the Unrequitable

"[O]nly the beloved can in this world bring about what our human limitations deny, a total blending of two beings, a continuity between two discontinuous creatures. Hence love spells suffering for us in so far as it is a quest for the impossible ...."

Georges Bataille, *Erotism: Death and Sensuality*

1.

I will not repeat
I will not repeat
I will not repeat

no ordinary excavation
become ordinary
become craven

the elixir's aftertaste
divines the elixir

it will not devolve

        [(h)e lie

             exire

     exit here]

elixir: he licks her (skin) (ellipsis) (denial)

while *her* sears *my*

2.

either the cleaving to
or cleaving from

argues an ague
for any hand that will

praise
is to pray

whose secular world?
whose Iron Age?

whence touch
whence chasm

hands and hands hover at the whole

3.

Descent might be merely the postponement of ascent

descent displacement or a return,
the abrupt shudder back into the self,
isolate for the cringe   *Oh*

Cutting daffodils will not
A call: *Other?*
Oh, here *you* are   Projected   And ever as

4.

your voice through the phone
        when I a girl of eight or nine
                why have you gathered them into
the desk lamp's small pool
the female spills spills
wet hands revel or shake
        did you have an imaginary
        the cornfields stretch into
wet with saliva and
        Mandy when I was eight or ten the cache of
                send any others
        eight to eleven or twelve
your voice did you have
                send them when the light spills
the cornfields by my house I was eight or nine
                a cache by definition does not leak or lose
                        lay down
        why did you bring else and other
drenched
don't wrench
        alone in the stalks except for

        what did you have   in that field
                sacrosanct alone and not alone
                alone and not alone you have that reservoir

5.

body
I scale

with a gaze
anodyne

for the ascetic
for the un-

toward the moss
green (iris)

toward is away
stained glass

(too high)
(too holy)

I scale
for the blur

heady
in incomplete

satis, enough
not yet not near

but my lips   *ooooooooooh*

the cusp is always air

6.

ether & ephebe
odi et amo

et amo
in the dissipating

enunciates touch
wrist & nape

lips for
the summons

(not to purse)
(not to part)

masculate toward
(that ether)

littlebeard my other
toward our

ether, ephebe

7.

sleet hiss instantiates all walls
horas ad dies ad
to touch is to torque the familiar or

the familiar heightens
perlucence death-borne the brief
hairs along the curve of your ear

sleet *susurrus*

8.

thigh to waist
azure all *thinking*

down the arc-stroke
up *cuts* the slow

cuts disappearing *furrows into*
the soil of skin

of Being
that azure infinite eyes & _____

9.

ante mare et terras et quod tegit omnia caelum
before the sea and the lands and the sky that covers all things

but itself the blur
of blooming clover

from the train
& trained eye

Ovid claims *ante*
the parcelled temporality of

thirteen hours later
you as if and so

here in the swash invisible

quem dixere Chaos

10.

lip to thigh break

into our indivisible

oak trunk wheel to axle

breathe to gasp the tumbling

clock's *a priori* but

given rib tibia cranium

under the skin the muscle

around the marrow inside

the bone that yet palm to

hip into all dishevelled

wandering stars

Divining for Starters (77)

The Swan, Bradford on Avon

syncopate to the possibility of

slow trumpet

if I nod I mean

eye you eye

pluck to pluck to

jazz—

heat cups my breasts

summer aesthetic

flirt me

eye you eye

double bass through

the old gentleman

cymbal-brush –brush

O to be a girl

abash and swing

my trumpet my drum my xylophone—

Poem for Two Voices (4)

What am I supposed to know?

                              the signs, the signals

Who?

                                        men

With or without wine?

                                 obviously

obvious to you

                                 transcribe

amanuensis

                           which is to translate

me and my tongue

                                yeah, yeah

delect

                                     able

desire

                                   able

amid the cacophony

the signs, the signals

O for an air traffic controller

a grammar for the nonverbal

sex and desire and

conversation

O for an unrequitable

it's all

amid the cacophony

lovable, legible

that'll do

III

Divining

Under beer and on the humid

Under beer and on the humid
sounds like distance stretching into itself
though, in unmeasured moments,
identifiable as semis on the interstate.
Looking away at the overgrown
and the equilibria lose novelty.
Fecund names the loss.
Pinioned relative to the imaginable,
pines never taller on either side of the field.
Yes, yes, the gnaw. Tonight
the barmaid refuses to apologise.

Election

When wind grazed the fields and the sun gave kaleidoscopes meaning, we rallied behind our candidates. There was dew on the hydrangea, and scientists recorded the emissions of stars. Hoping the contender's heart most resembled our own, each of us loitered at the voting booth, each of us used a foot to draw shapes in the sand. Within hours a near-apocalypse sundered elements and earth, and the election ended in pure democracy: a trio of voices with scripts for a sextet.

The Occupation of Iraq

Wounds under plaster or gauze are not wounds
to the beholder. These early daffodils come to bloom
and die in four days. The trick is to lose well,
which is not the same thing as losing profoundly,
not always. The swaddled wound appears already
on its way to recovery; it must, to preserve the pallor
of the bandage, have been washed clean, loose skin
trimmed. The idea was to fill the flat with buds
and leave for France. No bodily injury produces more pain
than that to the nerve, yet the eye cannot perceive it.
We left for France. The dentist overfilled
the canal, sent the sealant six millimeters into
the lingual nerve, delivered six hectares of misery.
On the first night, someone said *Canadienne* when I feared
Américaine, and I smiled. Winning comes with
a dictionary, all the right words without rules for syntax.
There is no exponent to relate my worst pain
to an entire country's wounds. We came back
from France, and the room was yellow with dying.
All we could see was loss.

Divining for Starters (68)

without the usual reassurances

at the fruit and veg stand

the errand enforcing

send it as printed matter

a day in the long vowel

dishes always dishes

blood is the course of it

breaking a glass against the tap

coarse risk

Savlon and Elastoplast

a handhold a foothold

a hand a foot   the human of it

Ache

would swell toward the limn

                          the division of time

ruptures the ripple

              casting toward an eclipse

    sorry oh sorry

                 the crouching I   abide

and bid and bid again

            casting for

              the division of here

     meant nothing exceptional

sure enough

      crouch and bide

            out of scent

compound and redound   redoubt

    bone bone bone

           monotonic

casting from an inevitable

     would would not   the division of body

      a cradle a softening (liquescence)

and hold   and hold

Divining for Starters (63)

at Salon Rosa, after the Berlin Wall Memorial

from the tall curtains' maroon-rich velveteen

at a loss to   where the light falls

the pattern gleams   which is to say

alienated   when one has so much practice in

the unscalable cliff face its sheer

put your finger on it   I forget how to sing

Divining for Starters (58)

sugar cube sugar cube
askance to a street
submerging as the clatter
of the restaurant below
recedes like my face
in a hall of mirrors
innumerable selves
and not a one

lipstick on the rim
salt and pepper in
small, silver pears
the wood chair not
the leather sofa
in which I'd sink
and thus moor

not cubes but rough clumps
whose lit grains glitter;
to widen in circles
from one point a
barely discernible rippling
toward the abstract
where there's no
pronoun for the self

sugar cube sugar cube

Poem for Two Voices (1)

This is the normative

not I

talking about a mode

of being?

I hadn't thought of that

which is to say

Did you see clouds scrape the spires?

mice in the fields

Live near cornfields, you want cats

normative is not

I never thought of myself as normal

or normative

Insignificance can't be normative

you would say

Cultivate beauty

like the young

Oh with them it just happens

leopard print

ageless

youth

ageless

normative

leopard print

normative

common

ordinary

ordinary

you would say

talking about a mode

sshhh

I'm cultivating beauty

naïve

I'm cultivating beauty

would that you were

shut up

we're not getting closer

it would be too easy

to ask what's normal

it would be too easy

complacency

normative

sacred

incandescent

yet recognizable

incandescent

        I'm not redefining

cultivated

        normative

I know that tune

(T)here

there I sang   always the equation   plenitude and
absence   daffodils a whole bobbing field
learning to disjoin   thoughtless   careless

lightning as the   ever-lagging illumination
of sound   down in the syllable   grunt and sway

a Saturday night   a beckoning thunder
a song a hymn   one man's chant

Saturday the pubs the   revving motorcycles
loudness   acceptably enjoyed   plenitude always
thoughtless   another attention   an ever sway

Divining for Starters (20)

deliquesce under mind over ear

tapering by degrees to the prick-peak

as if to stay the bell's toll

hail would be welcome the pain of

that satiety, bidden by breath

Divining for Starters (64)

in the humid weight late June

in the body ache and stretch

to contain the discord

there is no malice in it

leaping roof to roof until

so little binding force

why don't I wing

if it weren't for all these limbs—

Divining for Starters (16)

Out of the vernacular as the sky drains of light
The body heavy with a day's work that gravity
What would it mean to aspire to transcendence?

The garden more lush with encroaching darkness
The slight tremble of branches, call it a knowledge
Not the self—think of consciousness as steam

Dispersal and absorption; possessive adjectives aside
There's no knowing if willing it makes it so
Pooling again, with the drain and tremble

Something of appetite, of sensory reach
Reassumed, gravity grows lush, pooling

Divining for Starters (54)

once a summer the field was mown

a pub amid English voices faces architecture

with the coinage of the realm

sisters' weed-scratched sticks-for-legs

only then we remembered the baseball diamond beneath

ease and decline into memory

loud vowels locked in my throat and knocking

another, easier year

the mock-up of memory

just another American classic playing overhead

Divining for Starters (42)

from those barefoot days

a plateau in retrospect and occasionally in that time

someone's small-town pastoral, which is to say

the unbroken membrane of it

no one suspecting, no one heeding

acres of overgrown field

a strangely domestic elixir

snapping the pods off the vine and eating the peas raw

blithely someone's daughters

crest and crouch again

Divining for Starters (71)

in the quick of my wine

and trampling of sentiment

crucible of unrequited

walk down and down

nothing left to say

or there's no appeasing

tentative on the ice

beauty I'd have beauty

quick into dearth

the steep pitch

proclivity predilection intention

make of it *mi fabbro*

Divining for Starters (38)

in the last minutes of a vagrant day

supplicating in that guilt, the rain clamouring at the glass

where is desire, its sense of purpose

making no claims on my ability to render

not even songs, call them half-hymns

seeing through the streaks, amid the darkening

across the green, on the edge of the streetlamp's

no sound but for coursing water

a blurred figure, wandering towards

perhaps not clamouring but calling

a blurred figure I think I know

Divining for Starters (27)

when did the rain

I lean into the other, that handy trampoline

or I spill outward into the grey peace whirring

a few streaks on the pane

the absence of children in this building means

Sunday I walked through the Tithe Barn, wishing I could hear

wishing on the absent odour of hay

I would pay my tithe of rain to

the rain suspended in the air, a flickering curtain

feel the plea tug its way forward

in the absent in the faintest whir

A Starkness in Late Afternoon

afternoon light   on stone   is immediacy
thought or   in itself
immaculate unsundering

the geese's flight   their warm
indivisible bodies   as much as   on the path
coarse stone   a single feather

and here I go   tearing the quilt
apart   patch by patch   all parts
no one   no one will love

on the storm-   fed sea   the wrath
the men and I   all prey to
praying to   the sea god

the high waves could be   suppose it
myrmidons   unnamed abettors
our fear   unchanged unchanneled

our prayers   scattered invisible

Poem for Two Voices (2)

I began in depth

where's the paddling pool?

nuanced by contrast

making a handle

every time I retold the story

meaning keeps moving

colours grew sharper or changed

edging beyond the visible

upending the usual connotations

the story's colouring

creating new enigmas

had something to say

over and over again

a matter of habit

of circumstances

of need or a hunger for

the retelling

palimpsest

until I can't recall the original

if there is such a thing

palimpsest, the traces of erasure

an awkward transition, a

the unconscious decision

a kind of frame

in the starting point

feeling apologetic

once upon a life

for all thus lost

not *that* story

invented her own Golden Age

the stealth of recognition

in the retelling

what is depth?

the colour of

ambiguous all the same

River Seam

i.

Nightwatch sibilance

the phases of   plosives

     —O infidel

         the mundane the McDonald's   neon
      acting on the break

           another of the innumerable variables

sex and all that a body

        lavish cultivate   *puh puh*

    amid the other's   once upon a time

  puh puh pleez

ii.

the circus tent   the parade glitter and roar
                                    all the ecstasy of revelation

here becoming liminal   *I have to tell you that*
       waters waveheight wind

                    you know what I mean
                                        the potential expense
       of knowing the present progressive   of incalculable

                    fireweed for acres

iii.

small well-held vow

alongside the rising river the heft of sandbags
                            North already plundered
come down
    a letter an old newspaper a diary

    the words slow dissolve   *come down and try*

        the volume of volume
                the river of

iv.

    not to say there won't be

pulled taut   the stitches
                fixed and yet

      an economy of fluent motion   echolocate
        sundry I was sure

            infidelity at times denotes fidelity to

      promise   on the water
    enchanted I'm

      surely

Notes

In 'Subterfuge for the Unrequitable'—

The quotation from Bataille that precedes the poem derives from Mary Dalwood's translation, San Francisco: City Lights Books, 1986, page 20.

The opening phrase in section 6, *odi et amo,* comes from Catullus, poem n° 85, and means "I hate and I love".

In section 7, *horas ad dies ad* translates as "hours into days into".

The italicised sentence in section 8 is from Heidegger's essay, 'The Nature of Language', in *On the Way to Language,* translated by Peter D. Hertz (San Francisco: Harper and Row, 1982).

The words from Ovid in section 9 derive from *Metamorphose*s, lines 5 to 7. *Ante mare et terras et quod tegit omnia caelum* translates as "before the sea and the lands and the sky that covers all things", *ante* as "before", and *quem dixere Chaos* as "which was called Chaos."

The last four words of the final section are the last four words of Yeats's poem, 'Who Goes with Fergus?'

Acknowledgements

I am grateful to the editors of the following magazines, where many of these poems previously appeared (sometimes in earlier versions, occasionally with different titles): *Aufgabe, Bombay Gin, Cannot Exist, Damn the Caesars, Dusie, East Village Poetry Web, Faultline, Free Verse, Gists & Piths, Great Works, non, Oasis, Painted, spoken, Poetry Review, Poetry Salzburg Review, Poetry Wales, Shearsman, Slope* and *Tears in the Fence.* Thanks also to the editors of *Angel Exhaust, Arshile, Jacket, Nedge* and *Tenth Muse* for their publication of related work.

Some of these poems also appeared in the following chapbooks/pamphlets: *Subterfuge for the Unrequitable* (Potes & Poets, 1998), *Yet* (Leafe Press, 2008), and *Divinations* (Punch Press, 2010). Thanks to editors Peter Ganick, Alan Baker and Richard Owens for their interest and support.

On my arrival in England, Tony Frazer and the late Ian Robinson encouraged my writing in this vein and supported it with publication; Peter Philpott soon joined them. I cannot thank them enough. I also want to thank my family for their unwavering faith.

For their generous, rigorous attention to the manuscript, I am deeply grateful to Andrea Brady, Matt Bryden and Claire Crowther.